Butterflies
in My Garden

For information contact:
MONDO Publishing
980 Avenue of the Americas
New York, NY 10018

Visit our web site at http://www.mondopub.com

Printed in China

04 05 06 07 08 09   9 8 7 6 5 4 3 2 1

ISBN 1-59034-031-0

Butterflies
in My Garden

by Linda Bullock
Illustrated by Ann Barrow

MONDO

I have butterflies in my garden!

They are flying from flower to flower.

Their wings open and close.

They are black with orange, yellow, and blue spots.

What are these yellow spots on the carrot tops?
They look like little butterfly eggs.

Five days, ten days have gone by.

Where are the little eggs?

Oh, my. Are you a caterpillar?

You don't look like a caterpillar!

Three weeks, four weeks have gone by.

Now you look like a caterpillar!

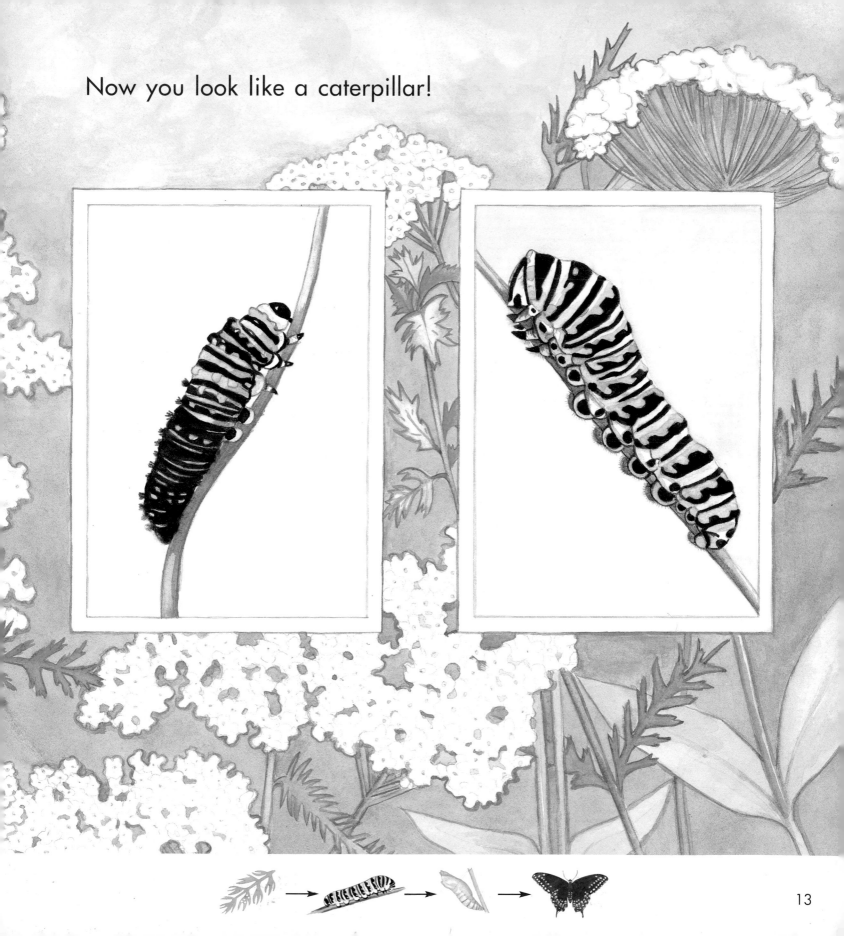

Where are you now?
You are inside!

chrysalis

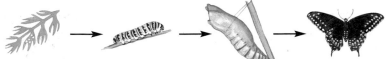

I have watched you for two weeks.

Are you coming out now?

Oh, my!

You look like your mother and father.

You are getting warm in the sunlight.

Look at you!

You are a butterfly.

Your mother and father lived in my garden.

Will you live here, too?

You can fly from flower to flower.

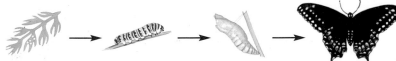

You can lay your eggs on the carrot tops.

Look! You did lay your eggs here!

I know what will happen now.

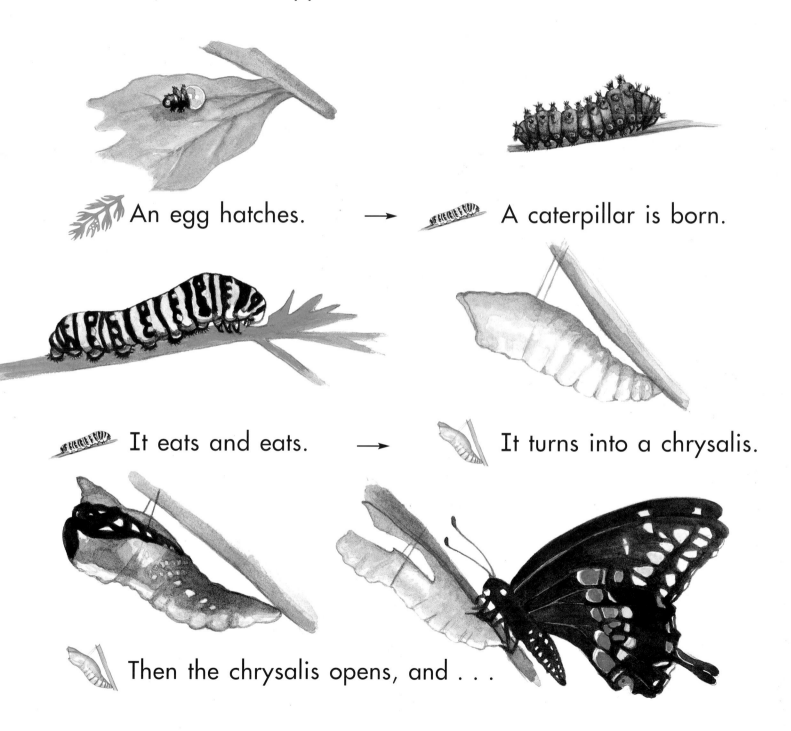

An egg hatches. → A caterpillar is born.

It eats and eats. → It turns into a chrysalis.

Then the chrysalis opens, and . . .

. . . a new butterfly lives in my garden!